Bar Exam Basics

A Roadmap for Bar Exam Success

Volume 1 in the

Pass the Bar Exam Series

Matt Racine

Editor, BarExamMind.com

Pass the Bar Exam Series

Book 1: Bar Exam Basics: A Roadmap to Bar Exam Success

Book 2: How to Write Bar Exam Essays: Strategies and Tactics to Help You Pass the Bar Exam

Book 3: Bar Exam Mind: A Strategy Guide for an Anxiety-Free Bar Exam

Book 4: The Bar Exam Mind Bar Exam Journal

Other bar exam resources available at BarExamMind.com

California Bar Exam Outlines

MBE Outlines

Table of Contents

Why You Should Read This Book

THIS BOOK PROVIDES you with the roadmap you need to make it through your bar exam preparations without worrying about taking a misstep that could cost you success on the bar exam. It does the thinking about the little details you need to take care of during a successful bar exam campaign.

By the time you finish this book, you should have a complete overview of the bar exam process and how it will affect your life for the next few months. With that knowledge in mind, you can set out to organize your studies to ensure you integrate them into your life, rather than allowing them to take over your life.

While you should never underestimate the bar exam, the bar exam is not as difficult as you may have been led to believe. If you believed much of the bar exam gossip, you might think the test is a massive, horned beast that only the most intrepid souls can defeat.

This is nonsense.

The bar exam is a test. It is based on information. It requires practice and preparation – nothing more, nothing less. This book tells you how to practice and prepare effectively. It will guide you in your bar exam journey.

Does reading this book guarantee you will pass? No, but it guarantees you will not make the same mistakes many people do which result in their failing the bar exam.

This is the book that I wish I had been able to read before I took my first bar exam.

It would have reduced a lot of my uncertainty and anxiety. Questions constantly swirled around in my head, distracting me from doing what I should have been doing to prepare for the test. Questions like:

- Am I studying enough?
- How should I study?
- How much do I need to practice?
- Will my family and friends understand how hard this is?
- What should I do on test day?

This book provides answers to these and other common questions and concerns about the bar exam.

And, who am I to write this book? I have taken and passed two bar exams: Oregon and California. When I took the Oregon bar, I was stressed out and freaked out. When I took the California bar, I applied what I learned from taking a previous bar exam to make the second experience much more streamlined and less stressful.

Since then, I have maintained two bar exam blogs – Bar Advisor and Bar Exam Mind – and counseled hundreds of bar exam students just like you through email, on the phone, and in person. I know what it takes to pass the bar exam, and I have seen what leads to failure.

This book contains what I believe is the most important information you need to know to pass the bar exam.

Let's get started.

Bar Exam Level Set

SOME PEOPLE UNDERESTIMATE how disruptive studying for the bar exam can be to their lives and the lives of their family and friends. It is important to think about this as soon as possible, at the outset of your studies if possible.

If you made it through law school flying by the seat of your pants, rushing from one fire to the next, and pulling a few all-nighters each month to play catch-up, it is time to get organized. A piecemeal approach to the bar exam just won't work.

Here is the deal: The bar exam is unknown territory for most people, and in my opinion, a big part of the stress and anxiety created by the bar exam has to do with the unknown. Because preparing for the bar exam is a long, time-consuming endeavor, you do not want to rush into it without some thought and planning.

With the bar exam, you are dealing with two unknowns: (1) the test itself and (2) its effect on your life and the lives of those close to you. I hope you will seriously consider what I have written in this chapter and will take the time to perform a **bar exam level set** to help make your life more manageable during the weeks and months you study for the bar exam.

What is a level set?

A "level set" simply means to assess your resources and your goals to see what you need to do or obtain in order to achieve those goals. So, a *bar exam* level set is an examination of available resources to help you pass the bar exam. The level set process may involve your friends, your significant other, your family, and anyone who you think could help *or hinder* your bar exam preparations.

I'll give you some broad categories to think about for your level set next, and then conclude this chapter with a checklist of specific items. Be sure to go through the checklist thoroughly so you do not neglect anything.

No. 1: Determine Where and When You Will Study

Do you need total silence when you study? Can you handle some noise but not too much? Are you easily distracted or could you study at a rock concert? The answers to these questions will determine where you should study.

Some suggested locations:

- law library (possible distractions from colleagues talking to you)
- public library (some can be loud)

- home (might not be a good choice if you have a loud roommate, children, or are easily distracted by other tasks like cleaning or gardening)
- coffee shop (I could never have done this, but some people seem to be able to pull this off)
- outdoors (study in a park? at the beach? maybe, but will you be able to focus?)

Once you have decided *where* you will study, you should determine *when* you will study. It is important to pick a schedule and stick to it. Many bar exam students suffer from "mission creep" and begin studying at all hours of the day and night. As I will explain in more detail in a later chapter, a chaotic schedule is detrimental to your ability to learn.

Some possible study schedules include:

8am to 5pm: I think this is ideal and it is how I studied for the bar exam both times that I took it. By following this schedule, you study at the same time the actual bar exam is administered, so you train your body and mind to be focused during the same time as the test. On the other hand, you need to be highly focused everyday while you study during these hours, and you generally can only take short breaks if you want to fit the necessary studying into these hours.

8am to 10pm (or similar, e.g., 6am to 8pm): This schedule allows you to take longer breaks while you are studying, maybe to exercise during the day or spend a few hours with your family. It is probably a good schedule for people who have commitments beyond simply studying for the bar. The main drawback I see is that the later at night you study, the harder it can be to fall asleep, and you need to get sleep while studying for the bar exam.

6pm to Midnight: This is a schedule for people who are working during the bar exam. Obviously, not ideal, but you have to do what is necessary. Having a late night schedule will likely require studying for a significant portion of the day during the weekends. But be sure to take breaks and get some good sleep. (I had a colleague who was working as a full-time attorney in California who was studying for the New York bar exam at night and on the weekends. She hated it, but she passed. Read her story at *barexammind.com/work-during-bar-exam-prep/.*)

Now that you have your basic study location and schedule decided, look at your calendar from now until the bar exam date. Determine if there are any large blocks of time when you will not be able to study.

For example, are there any commitments you cannot change during your bar studies that you will have to work around? Are there any important holidays that occur during your period of bar prep that you want to enjoy? Do you have any trips planned? Maybe a friend is getting married and you need to budget a few days to attend and enjoy the wedding? Figure this out now and account for it in your study schedule.

No. 2: Eliminate or Reduce Stressors and Potential Stressors

To the extent you can foresee a stressor that may negatively affect your ability to focus on your test preparation, you should try to do something *now* to eliminate the stressor or reduce the likelihood that it will have a negative effect.

Doing this may require some uncomfortable conversations with family and friends or working out agreements with people (e.g., for the next 2 months, we won't do "x", but after the exam is over, we'll do "x" every day for a week).

Some typical sources of bar exam stress include family, finances, and food.

Family

Do you have kids who will need attention? My kids were 1 and 3 when I took the Oregon bar exam, and 3 and 5 when I took the California bar. I made a commitment to think about the bar when I was at the library from 9 a.m. - 5 p.m. but then was fully present for them (and my often exhausted wife) when I was home.

Is your spouse or significant other needy? Will he or she be jealous of the bar exam for occupying so much of your time and attention? If you think this could be a problem, consider ways to reduce it. Some possibilities: Commit to a date night once a week; take Saturdays off and do something with your significant other; or promise to cook dinner a few nights a week.

Finances

You do not want to run out of money while you are studying for the bar exam. If you think you might run short on funds, cut back on expenses where possible. Possible places to reduce spending: Downgrade or cancel your cable subscription; cancel any monthly subscriptions to newspapers or websites; avoid buying new clothes; and try not to eat out too often.

If you find yourself a little short of money one month, there are lots of ways to get a few hundred dollars quickly. Do you have family you can tap for a couple hundred dollars if absolutely necessary? What about freelancing using skills developed before law school? Could you offer tutoring to local high school or college students? Do you have anything you could sell on Craigslist or Ebay? What about babysitting?

Make sure your bills get paid and you don't overdraw your bank account. (The only time in my life I bounced a check was when I was studying for exams one semester during graduate school; I literally forgot to deposit a paycheck. If only I had signed up for direct deposit....) If you have auto-pay for your bills, great; if not, consider setting it up. If you don't like auto-pay, put bill paying into your calendar on the 1st and 15th of each month so you won't forget.

Food

You should make an effort to eat healthy food while studying for the bar exam. Poor food choices (e.g., sugary or starchy foods) can lead to brain and body fatigue, poor concentration, and depression-like mood swings. Not what you want at this critical time. (If you want more information on this topic, I have an entire chapter devoted to it in my book, *Bar Exam Mind: A Strategy Guide for an Anxiety-Free Bar Exam*.)

But, eating healthily takes time because you have to cook most of your food. If you are worried about having enough time to cook, consider preparing meals in advance and freezing them. I have one friend who cooks five days' worth of chicken breasts, vegetables, and rice each Sunday. He separates the food into five Tupperware containers and freezes them so that he has his dinners for

Monday through Friday all ready to go. Kind of boring, but basically healthy.

Maybe you can get your significant other, a roommate, or a family member to cook for you? The mother of one colleague of mine actually moved in with her for the last three weeks before the bar exam. She cooked all her meals, washed her laundry, and cleaned her apartment.

Now that is love!

No. 3: Deal with Fear and Anxiety about the Bar Exam

Bar exam fear, stress and anxiety is the main focus of my Bar Exam Mind blog, and I won't go into great detail in this chapter. The point is, if you are worrying about the bar exam and consequences of failing the bar exam, it makes it more difficult to study for the bar exam.

To deal with the stressors of fear and anxiety, consider using negative visualization to put the fear in its proper perspective and positive visualization to build confidence. I explain these techniques and others in great detail in my *Bar Exam Mind* book.

Finally, if your fear or anxiety is so extreme as to be debilitating, consider seeking help from a therapist, psychiatrist or other mental health professional.

No. 4: Make Exam Day Preparations Early

Unless you happen to live a short walk from the bar exam testing site, chances are you will need to commute to the exam location or book a hotel room. I recommend spending the necessary money on a hotel room. It will give you extra down time and allow you a place to yourself to get away from the bar exam madness.

If you will need to commute to the bar exam site, be sure to have contingency plans in place in case your car does not start or public transit is delayed. For example, ask a friend to be on standby to drive you to the exam.

If you will be staying at a hotel, book your room as soon as possible. Most hotels will not charge your credit card until the day of your arrival, so this is an easy thing to do. Also, if you do book in advance, call the hotel a couple weeks before the exam and make sure that they have not lost your reservation. It *does* happen, so don't forget to double check. It is better to find out about this a couple weeks early rather than on the evening before the bar exam.

Level Set Checklist

In order to ensure that you consider the more detailed aspects of these areas, I am including a checklist for you to review. I have tried to make this checklist uber-comprehensive, so not all of the items will apply to everyone.

If you would like a free PDF copy of this checklist, just head over to *barexammind.com/bar-exam-level-set-checklist/* and grab it.

BASICS

- ☐ I have registered for the bar exam.
- ☐ I have completed all necessary paperwork for the bar exam, such as:
  - ○ bar exam application
  - ○ moral character paperwork
  - ○ background check
  - ○ other?
- ☐ I have paid all fees to be able to take the bar exam.
- ☐ I have purchased exam software if I am using a computer to take the test.

- ☐ I have signed up for the Bar Exam Mind newsletter at BarExamMind.com.

STUDYING

- ☐ I have determined *where* I will study.
- ☐ I have determined *when* I will study.
- ☐ I have signed up for a comprehensive bar exam prep course(s) (or individual tutoring).
- ☐ If I cannot afford a bar prep course, I have located affordable or free study materials.

FAMILY/FRIENDS

- ☐ I have spoken with my significant other about understanding my time commitment while studying for the bar exam.
- ☐ I have spoken with my significant other about how I may become very stressed out during my bar exam studies.

- [ ] I have worked out any scheduling issues with my significant other:
    - o Vactions
    - o Weddings
    - o Childcare
    - o Other?
- [ ] I have told my non-bar-taking friends that I may not be as available as before while I study for the bar exam.
- [ ] I have arranged for childcare, if necessary.
- [ ] I have spoken with my children about how important the bar exam is to me and how I may need some quiet time while I study.

FINANCES

- [ ] If I am concerned about money, I have cut back on unnecessary expenses.
- [ ] I have set up a system to ensure I pay my bills, in case I get so wrapped up in bar exam studies that I forget about them.
- [ ] I have set up auto-pay for my bills, if I think that will help.

- [ ] I have determined whether I will need any extra money to make ends meet while I study for the bar exam and have thought about how to obtain that money (e.g., loan, part-time job, freelancing, etc.).

FOOD/HEALTH

- [ ] I have thought of when I will shop each week for healthy food.
- [ ] I have thought about how I will make time to prepare healthy meals (e.g., I'll cook all my meals for the week in advance on Sunday).
- [ ] I have scheduled time to exercise during my studies.
- [ ] I plan to get a full night's sleep as often as possible.

EXAM DAYS

- [ ] I have made hotel reservations, if necessary.
- [ ] I have made travel arrangements.
- [ ] I have tested my exam software if I am taking the test on a computer.

Final Thoughts...

Passing the bar is difficult, but many people have done it. You can do this. Make the commitment to pass.

Get your life organized before you start studying so the only thing you need to worry about is studying. It may take some planning and negotiating, but it is important to make these arrangements now.

Don't let the stress and anxiety build up before you take action.

Creating Your Bar Exam Mindset

NOW THAT YOU HAVE thought about how to arrange your life while you study for the bar exam, I'll let you in on a little secret: The bar exam is not just about how much knowledge you have of the law.

The bar exam is really a test of how well you function under an extended period of stress. It is not only about the stress of taking the actual exam itself but also the stress of several months of preparation. This ongoing stress can lead to a negative mindset that can sabotage bar exam success.

This chapter is about creating a positive mindset to help you succeed on the bar exam whether you are a first-time taker or a repeater.

Growth vs. Fixed Mindset

Carol Dweck, a world-renowned psychologist at Stanford University, has determined through decades of research on success and achievement that there are two general categories of mindset: fixed and growth.

With a fixed mindset, one believes one's basic qualities, like talent, intelligence or ability in a particular area, are simply fixed traits. Such people spend their time *documenting* their talent or intelligence instead of striving to develop them. Their talents are verified when they get good grades, win awards and receive praise. They also believe (wrongly) that talent by itself creates success *without* effort.

I see the fixed mindset often in law students. Most of them have been good students throughout their lives, and many attribute this to their inborn talent and intelligence. They believe they are "smarter" than the average person and have excelled academically because of that superiority. When they have trouble academically or as they study for the bar exam, they tell themselves they are "stupid" or "won't ever get this stuff."

Contrast this to people with a growth mindset. Someone with a growth mindset believes his or her most basic abilities can be developed through hard work, dedication and perseverance. Intelligence and talent are a good foundation, but not nearly enough. People with a growth mindset tend to have much greater resilience and can endure more trying times and hardship to reach their goals.

So, which mindset do you have?

If you do not have a growth mindset, be alert for negative self-talk about being too stupid to learn a particular concept or incapable of learning how to write a bar exam essay. These are the expressions of a fixed mindset. You need to instill in yourself a growth mindset as best as possible.

As a long-time victim of a fixed mindset, I know how self-criticism can push you into a dark place. It takes constant vigilance to remain in the light of a growth mindset.

Establishing Your Mindset for the Bar Exam

There are lots of techniques for establishing a proper mindset. By "proper mindset," I mean a mindset that will support you in the achievement of desired goals rather than undermine you. You should do your best to encourage a growth mindset and a positive outlook on your day-to-day life as you follow your study routine.

Please note that "proper mindset" is not a one-size-fits-all concept. Some people may function better with a calm mindset focused on flowing with events, while others will function better with a mindset that views the world as one of obstacles to be overcome by force and struggle. Either of these can be manifestations of a growth mindset.

One difference between fixed and growth mindset seems to be that a fixed mindset manifests as a voice *speaking to* us, but with a growth mindset we *speak to ourselves*. For example, let's assume you are sixteen years old and you just failed your behind-the-wheel driver's licensing test. If you had a fixed mindset, you might hear a voice saying, "I can't believe what a terrible driver *you* are. Why did *you* even bother trying to learn how to drive?" But, if you had a growth mindset, you might say to yourself, "Gosh, that was harder than *I* thought it would be. *I'm* disappointed right now, but *I* will practice some more and pass the test next time."

When you recognize that your fixed mindset voice is belittling you about your bar exam studies, tell yourself that you are working hard and will soon learn what you need to learn. Replace any negative talk with positive statements or recall a time you worked hard for something and achieved a goal. It need not be an academic moment, but maybe something related to a sport or hobby you enjoy.

As recommended in my book, *Bar Exam Mind: A Strategy Guide for an Anxiety-Free Bar Exam*, you can also try using positive affirmations such as:

- I am relaxed and calm.
- My mind stores and recalls information with ease.
- My brain is healthy and efficient.
- I deserve success and happiness.
- I study for the bar exam easily and effortlessly.

Create a Study Routine

MOST PEOPLE OFFERING advice about how to pass the bar exam tell you to follow a study schedule.

I am no exception to this, and I believe that following a schedule – whether it is given to you by a bar review program or you create it yourself – is essential to bar exam success.

But, I am not sure I have ever seen anyone discuss the value of establishing a daily and weekly routine during your studies.

Routine vs. Schedule

To be clear, a routine is not the same thing as a schedule.

A **schedule** is a timetable that you follow so that you will complete certain tasks within a given time limit. For instance, if you choose to follow the study schedule given to you by the good folks from some bar preparation course, you will complete studying and practicing each of the bar exam subjects about two weeks before the bar exam. Then, you will use the remaining time to continue to practice and to review your weaker subjects so that you will be prepared when the exam begins.

A **routine**, on the other hand, should be thought of as the rhythm of your life. For example, my weekday routine is that I wake up around 6:00 a.m. each morning, drink a glass of water, exercise for 20-30 minutes, meditate for 20 minutes, take a shower, eat breakfast, get my kids ready for school, and get to work around 8:30 a.m. I work until 5:00 or 6:00 p.m., then I come home, eat dinner, relax, and go to sleep by 10:00 p.m. each day. Within this routine, I fit my daily work schedule. The schedule varies each day of the week, but my routine rarely varies.

Why Establish a Routine?

It is important to establish a routine because a routine provides stability, freeing you to concentrate on your studies.

In other words, a routine gets your mind and body into an expected rhythm. Any source of stability is important while you study for the bar exam because you are placing heavy demands on your brain to memorize voluminous material. The stability means that your brain has one less uncertainty to worry about as you continue on your bar exam journey.

With a strong, well-planned routine, you fit bar exam studying into your life, but the studying does not *take over* your life. This is extremely important because some students preparing for the bar exam report feeling overwhelmed, helpless and depressed because they cannot find time to spend with friends and family and seem to do nothing except study.

With a strong routine in place, you will be effective and focused when it is time to study, but will be able to relax and get away from the bar exam when it is not study time.

Unless you have to work during your bar exam studies, one possible bar exam routine could be: Wake up at 6:00 a.m., exercise, shower, get dressed, eat, commute to bar exam study location, attend lecture or study topic "x" per study schedule, lunch, practice topic "y" per study schedule, commute home, dinner, nighttime activities, in bed by 10:00 p.m.

In addition to the daily routine, you should establish a weekly routine. In the weekly routine, I highly recommend you take a minimum of one day off from studying and make sure you fill that day with something that will help recharge your mental batteries, such as spending time with friends, going for a hike, watching a movie, or just plain relaxing.

Breaks in the Routine

It is inevitable that you will have some breaks in your routine. Maybe you have a sleepless night; maybe the water heater at your house breaks in the middle of the night and you have to stay up waiting for the plumber. Life is like that.

But these breaks should be rare and will be things that are outside of your control. If there is a break in your routine, try not to worry. Assuming your routine is well-established, you should be able to get back into your routine quickly.

Don't Overstudy

BUT IT'S THE **BAR EXAM**. What do you mean don't overstudy? Is it even possible to overstudy for the bar?

Yes. Let me explain.

There are two main goals at the heart of bar exam study: (1) learn the substantive law you need to pass the exam and (2) learn how to take the test itself.

You can accomplish the first goal by enrolling in any good bar review course or by acquiring/buying the right materials to learn the law on your own. You accomplish the second goal by anticipating the format of the bar exam, taking practice tests, and building up your endurance for the marathon that is a two- or three-days-long bar exam.

But don't overtrain.

Exercise physiologists know that extreme exercising – such as weightlifting with no rest between sets and no days off *or* endurance training with no easy days or days off – can lead to injuries from overuse. Even worse, overtraining can sabotage performance at critical times. Too much running, for instance, can lead to slower race times rather than faster race times.

The same is true with bar exam preparation.

If you try and study 12-14 hours per day for 8 or 10 weeks straight, it will be very difficult to maintain your ability to learn. You will undoubtedly have days when your brain and body say, "Enough!" **You *will* hit the wall.** If you hit the wall too many times, it may impede your ability to succeed on the bar exam.

(*Note*: If you have a few days here and there where you can't seem to get much done, don't worry too much about it. This happened to me on occasion both times I took the bar exam. You just have to accept it, take some time – maybe a few minutes, maybe the rest of the day – off, and get back to studying when your brain wants to work again.)

Six Ways to Avoid Bar Exam Burnout

AS DEFINED BY WIKIPEDIA, "Burnout is a psychological term that refers to long-term exhaustion and diminished interest in work." I am no psychologist, but I have some specific ideas about how to avoid burnout when studying for the bar exam. I used these myself when I took the bar exam, and they worked for me. I hope they work for you.

In my opinion, there are six key ways to avoid burn out:

- Study during a predetermined block of time;
- Avoid distractions;
- Constantly test yourself;
- Take real breaks;

- Have fun when not studying; and
- Avoid obsessing.

Study during a predetermined block of time

One problem that leads to burnout is the feeling that you could be doing more. This applies in all areas of life. So, we need to make sure that we have some ways to cut this feeling off.

If you commit to studying during a set period of hours, then you can be more productive during those hours. Establish your study routine and stick to it.

In an ideal world, you would study during the hours when the bar exam is administered (roughly 8 a.m. to 5 p.m.). This way, you train your mind and body to care about the bar exam during those hours. Of course, some people work or have other commitments, and so will need to study during other periods of the day.

With many bar exam programs now featuring on-demand lectures, there is a temptation to study at all hours of the day and night. This convenience may seem like a great benefit, but it can easily lead to burnout. If you allow yourself to watch lectures late at night, or do practice questions at midnight, you keep your body under stress all day long.

Avoid distractions

If you are going to limit yourself to a bounded period of time to study, you need to focus during those limited hours. If you are distracted during that time, then you will not be making the best use of that time.

Eliminate all distractions over which you have control.

Put your phone on silent or leave it somewhere you cannot get to it without having to make an effort (e.g., keep it in your car when you go into the library to study). Do not use social media while studying. If you can't control yourself, use one of the many programs now available to automatically disable your ability to go to certain sites, such as Anti-Social, RescueTime or Freedom.

You only have limited mental energy each day. Don't waste it on distractions.

Constantly test yourself

Learning should be active. The best way to learn a concept is not to watch a video lecture for the third time, but to *apply* the concept you do not understand.

Write a practice essay. Take some targeted MBE questions and review the answer explanations until you understand them.

Passively reading through outlines does not get you very far. In fact, it can be so boring, that you will be compelled to check Twitter or text someone about how bored you are.

One good form of active learning is retrieval practice. Retrieval practice is quite simple: you study whatever you need to learn, then you take some time immediately after study to try and recall everything you just studied, then you compare what you remembered with what you studied to see what you missed, then you do another retrieval practice test.

For example, if you are studying Civil Procedure, you might read the part of your outline that deals with subject matter jurisdiction, then try to retrieve it from memory, review, then try retrieving again. Then, move on to the next sub-topic.

Take real breaks

I knew some people who never took a real lunch break when they studied for the bar exam. They would review an outline or do flashcards while they ate.

Please, don't do this.

If you have been studying in a focused way prior to your lunch break, then your brain deserves a break. Go outside, each lunch on the grass, eat lunch with friends. The student lounge at my law school had a pool table. When I took my bar exam study lunch break, I often played pool with classmates.

Studies show that your brain needs these rest breaks to solidify learned information.

Have fun when not studying

This is not a new concept.

As Lord Chesterfield wrote to his son in 1739: "One should always think of what one is about; when one is learning, one should not think of play; and when one is at play, one should not think of one's learning."

I know it is easy to worry about the bar exam. I've done it myself. And, I was motivated to write my book, *Bar Exam Mind*, to help people get over bar exam worry and anxiety. A good way to avoid the worry is to let yourself have fun when you are not studying.

Exercise, hang out with friends (and don't whine about the bar exam), spend time with family (and don't whine about the bar exam), read a novel or two, see a movie . . . whatever, just make sure you have fun.

Avoid obsessing

This is similar to "have fun when not studying," but is broader. In addition to not obsessing while you are *not* studying, avoid obsessing while you *are* studying.

This is especially the case when you first begin your studies. You will get things wrong. You will make mistakes, whether it be with the MBE or with bar exam essays.

So what?

Just keep up with your focused studying, avoid burn out, and work on developing your growth mindset. Everything will work out. You will know enough and you will pass the bar.

Anticipation of Conditions

IN ORDER TO help you succeed on the bar examination – or any important test of ability – you should prepare for it under conditions approximating that "test" situation.

The more familiar the testing process is to you before the actual examination, the less likely you will be surprised by the intensity and time constraints of the bar exam itself. Once you get used to the format of the bar exam, you only need to worry about being able to recall the material (which is certainly enough!) instead of being stressed about finishing essays or MBE questions within the allotted time.

Anticipation of conditions is one of the reasons people in the military have live-fire exercises and combat training. You don't just hand someone a gun, drop him off in enemy territory, and say, "Go to it." A soldier needs to get used to the sights, sounds, and smells of a warzone until these become "expected" or "normal," so he may then perform the tasks his commander desires without a second thought for the situation in which he is being asked to perform. While failure on the bar exam has much less drastic consequences than failure in a war zone, there are lessons to be learned from the intense and cinematic preparation an advanced military undertakes.

The bar exam is, for many people, a highly stressed two- or three-day period. For some takers, it may be the most stressful situation they have ever been in. Therefore, understanding what the test will be like and practicing in similar conditions is of utmost importance. By rehearsing the experience of the bar exam under test-like conditions, you can reduce a large amount of the stress and anxiety you might otherwise feel on the days of the exam.

There are two central aspects of the bar exam for which one must prepare: (1) performing at a high level for 6-8 hours for two or three days in a row and (2) performing while surrounded by hundreds or even thousands of people who are frantically taking the same test you are.

Endurance and High-Level Performance

A bar exam is a multi-day affair. To my knowledge, all states require at least two days of testing, and several (like California) require three. For those in Louisiana, the test is also three days, but it is spread over a week (i.e., Monday, Wednesday, Friday). In order to give your best efforts during each day of the test, you should practice performing during a multi-day testing situation.

Many large bar preparation programs will build in to the course schedule a mock bar exam where you show up at a designated site and take a test in the same format and under the same time constraints as if you were taking your jurisdiction's real bar exam. This is great and, if you take the test seriously, will likely be sufficient preparation under the endurance prong of my suggestions to you.

By "take the practice test seriously," I mean that you should show up, give your best effort for the full time allowed, and get used to the intensity of the exam. Unless you are brilliant, your performance on the practice test will likely not be a passing effort. But that does not matter because the point here is just to see how your body and mind reacts to being forced to test for several days in a row.

For those of you not taking a bar review course that includes a sample bar examination, you need to build such practice into your study schedule.

When I took the Oregon bar, I was taking BarBri and so used its practice test. When I studied for the California bar exam, I was doing it on my own and so had to build it in. I chose a Tuesday and a Wednesday as practice exam days, about three weeks before the actual February bar exam.

I only did a two-day practice exam even though the California bar exam is a three-day exam. I chose to do this for two reasons: (1) I had taken a bar exam before and was confident that if I could perform for two days, I could perform for three and (2) day three of the California bar has a format identical to day one, so I felt that studying rather than doing a practice test would be a better use of that extra day.

Another important thing to note is that I made the practice exam Tuesday and Wednesday. In most states, the bar exam starts on a Tuesday, and California is no exception. Furthermore, in states that use the MBE, it is *always* administered on a Wednesday. Therefore, to anticipate the conditions properly, I practiced the written portion on Tuesday and practiced the multiple choice MBE portion on Wednesday. Had I chosen to do a three-day practice exam, I would have done the second day of written practice on Thursday.

It is important to match the day of the week with the appropriate exam format so that your mind and body synchronize their abilities with the correct days of the week.

Finally, find out the approximate start time of your state's bar exam. Be sure that you start and stop your practice examination within those time parameters so that the practice session is as realistic as possible.

Practicing for Testing at the Testing Center

Once you have practiced for the endurance aspect of the bar exam, you need to practice for the auditory and visual experience of the bar exam. What I mean is that you need to be ready to take a test in a room with hundreds or thousands of people, many of whom are panic-stricken and hyper-stressed.

Let me briefly describe my two bar exam experiences:

For the Oregon bar, there is only one testing location for the entire state. All 700-1000 people taking the bar converge on a single location which, when I took the Oregon bar exam, was a rented convention hall at a hotel by the Portland International

Airport. The majority of these people take the test on a computer and are placed in the same room.

When I took the test, the computer-takers' room had probably 500 people in it. Prior to the test starting, the power suddenly went out to a large portion of the room because the drain on the daisy-chained extension cords set up by people apparently unfamiliar with electric circuits was too great. My laptop battery would only last about 2 hours. *Good thing I practiced hand-writing essays.* When the power went out, panic spread. Finally, the power was restored and the test started about 30-45 minutes late.

Once everyone was finally able to begin the test and start typing, it sounded like a heavy rain was falling inside the room. Thank goodness I had my earplugs in and that I had written most of my practice essays while wearing earplugs. The entire time I was typing

I kept wondering if the power would go out. I kept checking my power cord to ensure the green "it's still working" light was glowing. What a distraction! Day two was better since we only needed pencils to take the MBE. There was still panic in the air and a few people actually did not bother to show up for the second day, assuming they had failed.

In California, the number of people taking the exam requires that the bar examiners have several locations to administer the bar. I took it in San Diego, where it seemed like there was a mere 800 or so people in a convention hall taking the test on their computers. I have heard that some locations of the California bar have nearly 2,000 people taking the test.

With the California bar, the examiners seemed much more strict than those in Oregon. We had to put all of our test supplies in a clear plastic bag and leave our backpacks outside of the room. We had to provide fingerprints, signature cards, and photo ID during various moments of the exam. Just silly junk, but distracting nonetheless. At least I did not have to sit through the earthquake that hit during the July 2008 examination!

As you can see, any manner of things — anticipated and not anticipated — can occur at the bar exam. For example, during the North Carolina bar exam in July 2012, power was lost with the result that the air conditioning went out and laptop batteries eventually started to die, forcing many to handwrite the remainder of the exam.

If you practice under less-than-ideal conditions, then it is more likely you can adapt to the expected and unexpected distractions and stress that will occur during the actual bar exam.

In light of all these possibilities, I suggest that you set aside at least one block of time to practice essays (and, if your bar requires it, performance test writing) and another block of time to practice MBE questions (unless you are in one of those states that doesn't use the MBE; in that case, double your essay/PT prep). Then, locate a place where there will be a sizeable number of people who will be making at least some noise but where you will not likely be interrupted by someone speaking to you. Ideal places include a busy public library or a coffee shop.

Then, go to your chosen place and write an essay or a PT under timed conditions and then do 33 MBE questions in one hour. Try to do this on two or three separate occasions. Consider using at least one of the essay/PT writing sessions to practice handwriting the exam as well. Of course, be sure to do these practice sessions at the time of day when you would actually be doing the same thing for the bar examination.

Lastly, if your bar has odd rules for its exam, be sure to incorporate them into your anticipation of conditions practice. For example, the Virginia Bar requires that applicants take the bar examination wearing business attire. How would you like to fail because you weren't comfortable taking a test in a coat and tie (men) or wearing a tailored skirt or suit (women)? Do not let yourself fail for a foolish reason and for lack of practice.

In summary, make sure you do a complete test under timed conditions and practice bite-sized portions of the bar exam under unfavorable conditions. It will make a huge difference during the actual test.

Bar Exam Essays:

Basic Tips

[**Note:** If you would like to read my detailed discussion of how to approach the essay portion of the bar exam, please read my book, *How to Write Bar Exam Essays: Strategies and Tactics to Help You Pass the Bar Exam.*]

* * *

THE PROPER WAY to write an essay will depend greatly on the jurisdiction in which you take the bar examination. Your jurisdiction will also affect how you should prioritize studying for the essay portion of the exam.

The first thing to look at is how much the essay portion counts toward your total grade. If it is less than 30%, then you can probably make it your lowest priority. If it is over 50%, then it should be your highest priority. If it is somewhere in between, then you should adjust accordingly.

The second factor is to determine what are the time and length constraints for responding to an essay. For example, when I took the Oregon bar exam, I was given 90-minute blocks during which to write three essays, which works out to 30 minutes per essay. This is not a lot of time to digest a 1/2- to 1-page long fact scenario and write a good essay. The Oregon bar examiners realize this and so have imposed page/character limits. If you handwrite the exam, you get three pages; if you type the exam, you get a maximum number of characters which works out to almost exactly one single-spaced typed page. In such a situation, issue-spotting and rule statements are most important, while analysis will be kept to a bare minimum.

In contrast, in a jurisdiction like California, you have 60 minutes per essay and no page limit. Thus, even if you take an excruciatingly long 10 minutes to read the fact scenario and outline your essay, you still have 50 minutes to write. This is why some of the sample answers posted on the bar website read like law review articles. With that much time for each essay, analysis becomes king. While it is important to spot all the issues and explain the legal rules applicable or potentially applicable to the situation, if the analysis is lacking, it seems very likely – if not certain – that you will fail the essay portion.

Lastly, get your hands on copies of real essays that have been submitted and graded.

Read a few (3-6) from varied subjects before you ever practice writing an essay so that you can get a sense for the preferred response format in your jurisdiction.

When I took the Oregon bar, the BarBri course book had copies of actual graded essays. These were invaluable for at least two reasons: (1) demystifying the process of what gets points from the bar graders and thus lowering stress and (2) seeing that some pretty bad essays earned passing grades which raised my confidence level.

In California, for example, you can see copies of very good examination essays answers on the California bar website. These can be intimidating because many of them are extraordinarily well written. In addition, most bar preparation courses provide you with sample responses. (If you are taking the California bar exam, be sure to check out my review of BarEssays.com at *barexammind.com/review-of-baressays-com/.)*

So, determine where you can get copies of sample essay responses to help you prepare for the bar exam.

Applying the Information

Now that you have gathered all of the background information necessary to get the "lay of the land" for your jurisdiction's essay portion of the examination ... how to study?

As I indicated above, this will depend on the jurisdiction. So, I'll describe two study formats: (1) jurisdictions where analysis is minimal (e.g., Oregon and other states using the Multistate Essay Exam) and (2) jurisdictions where analysis is at a premium (e.g., California).

But first, one thing that is the same no matter where you take the exam is that you need to write out lots of practice essays. I'd recommend *at least* 2 per subject and be sure to do more for your weaker subjects, which amounts to about 30 practice essays *at a minimum*. You should write these sample essays under varying situations, such as writing a Criminal Law essay immediately after studying Criminal Law for 3 hours and writing a Criminal Law essay a week later after not having studied the subject for several days. Write essays in blocks under timed conditions simulating your jurisdiction's examination.

As you become comfortable with the essay format and feel that you can get all your thoughts down within the time limit, you can switch to simply outlining responses rather than writing out full-length essays. But, **do not switch** to outlining only until you are highly competent with writing out full-length essays!

Minimal Analysis Jurisdiction

As I mentioned, the premium in a Minimal Analysis Jurisdiction is on issue spotting and setting forth the applicable rule(s) of law. Therefore, ability to spot issues is the most important thing.

When you are at the beginning of your bar preparation and are practicing essay writing, be sure to spend an overly long period of time ferreting out every possible and tangential issue from the fact pattern. Write out a basic outline containing all the issues you can find. You can use sample essay questions from other jurisdictions to do this as well, since issue spotting is the same no matter who gives the test.

Of course, during the first few weeks of your studies, it is highly unlikely you will be able to spot all the issues in any given fact pattern because you will not have memorized enough law to do so. This is OK; give yourself permission not to be perfect because, after all, no one is.

The key with the intense issue spotting practice is to learn how the bar examiners in your state "hide the ball." In other words, you need to start learning which fact patterns are common for particular issues, which issues seem to always or almost always appear together, and how the differing "calls of the question" relate to the information appearing in the fact pattern.

If your jurisdiction imposes a page or character limit for essay answers, make sure you practice paring down your writing to get all the necessary information in to that length. This can be difficult, especially when writing an essay where the various issues have numerous subparts (e.g., constitutional law, torts, criminal law). During the first few weeks of practice, feel free to exceed the limit. The important part to begin with is to get all of the issues, rules, and analysis in written form.

Once you feel comfortable doing that, begin to edit yourself. Review examples of actual passing essays to see what information is necessary and is rewarded with points as compared to what information is superfluous and not point-worthy.

During the final two or three weeks before the examination, practice writing as many essays as you have time to write and then thoroughly *review*. Writing for its own sake is not enough, you must make time to review your essay responses and be sure you are truly learning or have learned the material. If you feel you have mastered writing complete essays, then review as many essay questions as possible to practice issue spotting.

Premium Analysis Jurisdiction

What I wrote in the first paragraph under "Minimal Analysis Jurisdictions" applies here as well. The first couple weeks are to learn how to issue spot – in my opinion, you should resist, during the first week or two of your bar prep course, the temptation to start writing out full-length essay answers. Writing out essays during the first week just induces frustration and anger. You are so overwhelmed at that point that writing bad essays (and they will be bad during the first few weeks) may send you over the edge into self-doubting oblivion.

Unlike with the Minimal Analysis Jurisdictions, the trick with a jurisdiction that gives you a large time allowance and no page limit is to build up stamina. For example, if you spot 5 main issues (each with, *of course*, multiple sub-issues) in a fact pattern, then you are going to have to write a lot in one hour to provide a thorough analysis. In order to build up the stamina (mental and physical) to accomplish this, you will need to have practiced writing numerous full-length essays under exam-like time pressure.

Building up stamina is something which must be done *over time*. After all, you don't learn how to complete the IronMan Triathalon with one week of training.

In addition to building up stamina, writing essays in a Premium Analysis Jurisdiction requires a much greater depth of knowledge than in a Minimal Analysis Jurisdiction. The greater depth of knowledge is necessary so that your analysis will be complete. If you have enough knowledge, your essays will often be extraordinarily lengthy and even one hour may not seem like enough time to write a response.

The only way to get this depth of knowledge is to study your bar prep materials a lot and know them cold. Honestly, though, this will not be accomplished by reading each outline 500 times. In order to truly learn the bar exam subjects, you need to *apply* the knowledge in practical ways, which include writing out and then reviewing numerous essays, developing issue checklists that make sense to you, and explaining concepts to yourself orally (do this where no one will hear you and think you are a raving lunatic).

In short, learn the information and then solidify it through application.

Advice for Writing Performance Tests

TO START WITH, there are two kinds of Performance Tests: the Multistate Performance Test (MPT) and a state-specific performance test, such as the California Performance Test (CPT). Both are essentially the same format, except the MPT is only 90 minutes while the CPT is 3 hours. Although I am unsure of exact totals, at least 33 jurisdictions (66% of them) use the MPT. If you plan on taking the test in a non-PT jurisdiction, consider yourself lucky.

I have passed both the Oregon and the California bar exams, so I have experience with both forms of PT.

The Oregon bar exam uses the MPT. I found the 90 minute format to be comparatively easy. There is only so much you can do in 90 minutes. In contrast, the 3-hour format of the California bar PT is onerous and, as a lawyer might say, overbroad as to time and scope.

The performance test is, allegedly, designed to test how you can think and write as a "real lawyer." I'm not so sure this is true since no "real" lawyer would digest 3-5 cases, review an entire litigation file, and draft and finalize a memo in 90 or 180 minutes. At least, I hope no real lawyer would do this.

Still, since most performance tests involve some sort of lawyer-like task (e.g., drafting a memo, preparing a letter to a client, preparing questions for a witness), if you have any experience doing this as a law clerk or summer associate, you will likely have an easier time with the PT than if you have never done these things.

As with all portions of the bar exam, the key to success on the PT is practice. To be successful, practice must be done in an efficient and useful way. Let me lay out the steps I suggest you to go through as you advance in your bar preparation.

General Preparation

Step 1: Before you do anything else, make time to read at least two examples of PT questions and answers. This will give you a sense for how the diverse information contained in the Library and File portions (discussed below) of the performance test materials get converted into a passing answer. For those of you taking the California bar exam, you can get some examples on the California Bar website. For those of you taking the MPT, you will probably have to rely on sample answers provided by your bar prep course. You can also get free copies of prior MPTs and grader point sheets from the National Conference of Bar Examiners website.

Step 2: At the proper time in your study schedule – say two weeks after you start, do your first practice PT. Do not write the answer out, but merely outline the answer. Then read the sample answer and see how much of the information you gathered and how closely you put the information and analysis in the correct order. You probably missed a few things. That's okay, make a note of what you missed and take the time to figure out why. This is the key: self-knowledge and understanding of your errors. You can plow away and write 30 sample PTs, but if you never review and learn, you will have much less success.

Step 3: Next, at the proper time in your study schedule – maybe six weeks before the bar exam, write out an entire PT. I would suggest doing a maximum of five sample PTs in their entirety. I think I probably did five when I took the Oregon bar and three when I took California.

For me, writing out an entire PT is soul-killing. The PT has nothing to do with memorization or knowledge and everything to do with how you spot relevant pieces of information. So, once you can do that, there really is no need to practice writing them out.

The real reason to practice writing PTs is to make sure you can get the job done within 90 minutes or 3 hours. In other words, you need to practice writing out entire PTs only until the point when you know the time pressure is no longer an issue for you. Then, you can just review PT tests periodically and do outlines to make sure you can spot all the relevant facts and legal authority. That said, if you have done five sample PTs and still are having trouble finishing within the time limit, then make sure you practice a few more.

Okay, so now I have given you the high-altitude overview. What about the neighborhood map? In other words, how do you write one of these things?

How to Write a Performance Test

Here is my approach. Think about it, try it once. If it works for you, great; if not, try to figure out why not and then modify it to suit your style.

The PT consists of a File and a Library. The File contains the assignment memorandum, format guidelines, and the facts you need to complete your task. The Library contains the various legal authority (statutes and cases, usually) you need to interpret those facts.

First, read the assignment memorandum in the File. This is the most important document. It will tell you *exactly* what to write in your response. Often, it can serve as an outline of the main topics you must discuss.

Second, skim (spend a max of five minutes) the entire Library, looking for anything that might be useful (e.g., multi-pronged tests, key words in statutes, etc.). Put a check mark in the margin next to these useful bits.

Third, skim (again, max 5 minutes) the entire File, noting facts that seem to relate to the assignment memorandum and the Library. Put check marks in the margins by these apparently important facts.

Fourth, read the assignment memorandum and the format guidelines memo (if there is one) carefully. Write down the major topics in basic outline format on a separate sheet of paper. [Note: Some people who type the exam will type the outline into their computer and then fill in the written portion of the PT. Although I typed both of my bar exams, that system did not work for me. If it did, I probably would have used it as it seems to increase efficiency and permit more time to write.]

Fifth, read the Library carefully and fill in your outline with the various legal tests and statutory language that is relevant to the topics you generated by reading the assignment memorandum. If necessary, re-write your outline on another sheet of paper.

Sixth, read the File carefully for facts applicable to the legal authority you have culled from the Library. Write in the appropriate place in your outline the basic fact and a citation (i.e., the page number so you can find it again) to that fact.

Seventh, review the outline and make sure it makes sense. If anything seems confusing, find the needed information to remove the confusion so that you can write a cogent response. [By now, a *maximum* of half your test time should have expired.]

Eighth, with your outline complete, start writing. If, as you write, you realize that you have left something out, I would suggest you make a note of it but then finish writing your entire PT so that you get a complete response. Then, if you have time left, you can search for whatever information was missing.

Pro Tip: When you start writing, be sure to write your conclusion first. That way, if something happens and you run out of time, it will look like you concluded your response, which should help you get a few extra points.

Advice for Taking the MBE

HERE IS A SECRET the bar examiners don't want you to know: The MBE is really a test to determine how well you take a test!

The MBE is not a test that tests only knowledge. If bar examiners wanted to test knowledge only, then the essay portion would be sufficient. After all, if you cannot explain something in writing, then (absent some sort of disability that leaves you unable to express your thoughts in writing) you likely do not understand it.

Now, I will admit that if you do not know the underlying law, then you cannot pass the MBE, so some knowledge is required. But, even if you have sufficient knowledge to write great practice essays, you may still struggle with the MBE. I know it was that way for me. That is why I think the MBE is really more about learning to pierce the veil of the MBE question-writing format than about how well you understand the legal subject areas tested.

A test to test your test-taking ability

What do I mean by this? In my opinion, the MBE is designed to trick you. The answers to many of the multiple choice questions turn on minor distinctions which the question narrative or fact-pattern make as opaque as possible.

Both times I took the MBE (in Oregon and California), I left the testing center with an uncertain feeling. I did not necessarily feel like I failed, but I had no idea if I passed. I thought I had answered many of the questions correctly, but I also thought that I had gotten many of them wrong.

The important thing, therefore, is to practice as many questions as possible, within reason. Thousands of questions would be ideal, though not always practical for some. Therefore, take the time to review all questions you get wrong so that you can learn from your mistakes.

When I studied for the Oregon bar and used PMBR (now called Kaplan), I did about 1500 of the questions. When I studied for the California bar, I used Adaptibar and completed every single one of the Adaptibar questions (I believe 1250 at that time) and then did a few hundred of the BarBri questions as well.

I preferred Adaptibar because it used real MBE questions released from previous exams. You can also get real questions, though fewer of them, in the *Strategies and Tactics for the MBE* books, which I highly recommend.

When I first started practicing MBE questions, my pass rate was between 25% and 40%, depending on the subject area. By the time the examination rolled around, I had a pass rate on the practice questions in excess of 80%, so I figured that I would be able to pass the real thing. Since I passed the bar exam both times I took it, I assume I at least did average on the MBE, though I suspect my actual score was above-average.

Practicing

So, you plan to do in excess of one thousand MBE questions? Good.

Now, how do you organize all this practice?

If you are enrolled in a bar preparation course and intend to follow the schedule you have been given, then just follow the schedule and you should get sufficient practice. If you are going to modify the bar prep course schedule or have created your own study schedule, then my suggestion is to do 25-40 questions for each subject whenever you have set aside time to do MBE questions.

So, for example, if you have set aside 2 hours to study Constitutional Law MBE questions, then do as many questions as you can in 90 minutes, and then take the last 30 minutes for review. Since the MBE is geared to finishing about 33 questions per hour, you should initially get through at least 40 questions in 90 minutes and should be at about 50 questions per 90 minutes when you approach exam time.

The important part of your practice is the **review**. I cannot stress this enough.

Let me repeat: The important part of practice is the **review**.

When you get a question correct, skim the answer explanation to make sure that you got it right because you understood the question, not because you got lucky. If you got lucky, then follow the "review protocol" explained below.

For the questions you missed, follow this error review protocol:

- read the answer explanation carefully;
- review the text of the question to see if – bearing the explanation in mind – you understand where you went wrong;
- determine if you were tricked by the question or if you simply did not know the rule, test, or theory being tested [if you were tricked, spend a minute understanding what exactly tricked you; be on the lookout for such tricks in the future]; and
- if you did not know the rule, then write a *flashcard* so that you can review that rule repeatedly in the coming days/weeks before the bar exam [don't overdo the flashcards;

you probably should try to limit the new ones to 5 per review session].

Endurance

You need to follow the same system every time you practice the MBE questions. Consistency creates familiarity which leads to proficiency and therefore bar passage.

As you review your study outlines and checklists, be cognizant of the areas with which you are having problems while studying for the MBE. Slow down when you review these portions of your outlines and checklists so that when you come across this area of law during your exam practice, you will engrave the concepts into your mind and have full command by the time the exam rolls around.

As another component of endurance, make sure that you follow my suggestion from the earlier chapter to take a full-length MBE practice test under timed conditions. This means a 200 question test, broken up into a 3-hour session for the first 100 questions, a one-hour lunch break, and then another 3-hour session for the second 100 questions. Make sure you do this at least two weeks before the real bar exam to get used to the time pressure.

And, of course, make sure you review all of your answers.

One Weird Trick?

A friend of mine from law school, Judy Parker, told me about her MBE testing technique. I think it is crazy, but she swears by it. I posted it on my blog, and I have gotten some really positive feedback. One reader even said it stopped him from getting the migraines he used to get when doing MBE practice. I include it here for your consideration:

First, I studied like normally, but I took careful stock of how well I was doing on each of the MBE sections.

When I took the MBE itself, I did **not** rush through question by question, but instead identified the typology of each question – I wrote a letter over each question in highlighter –T for Torts, E for Evidence, etc.

Then once all 100 questions were identified, I went section by section, doing all the Ts at the same time; then the Es, etc.

(Naturally, the self-analysis I had done earlier that summer allowed me to hedge which sections would be stronger for me and which I had a harder time with. If I could answer five torts questions correctly in the same time it took me to answer one property question correctly, why wouldn't I do so?)

In my opinion, the bar is designed to frustrate the takers and throw the takers off as much as possible. My plan mitigates that.

It also mitigates the strong psychological effect of having everyone in the room look at the same first ten questions all at the same time – someone is sure to make little moans or be happy with those questions and it throws others off. My plan makes you focus on categorizing what is right for you rather than what others are doing.

I took about one or two practice exams using this method and I guarantee that the time it takes to categorize is more than made up in the ease of staying within all the same types of questions – your mind doesn't have to switch back and forth 100 times, but only six times, from subject to subject.

As weird as it sounds, it makes a lot of sense. If I had to take the MBE again, I would seriously consider using it, though I'd be a bit scared about filling in the wrong bubbles.

The Last Few Weeks

THE FINAL TWO OR THREE WEEKS before the bar exam are critical. This is when everything you have been learning finally comes together and you will realize that you have learned enough to pass the bar exam.

Most bar exam preparation courses end two or three weeks before the bar exam so that you can use those final two weeks to focus on memorizing and practicing everything that you have been taught by your bar prep provider.

Switch into memorization mode

During your bar exam preparations leading up to the final two or three weeks, you have been attending bar exam lectures (either in a classroom or virtually); have been getting familiar with bar exam subjects, including subjects you may not have taken during law school; have been creating bar exam outlines and flashcards; and getting familiar with the structure of bar exam testing, including practicing essays, performance tests, and MBE questions.

All that information can be overwhelming at times. Just finding the time to make your outlines or flashcards or to review lecture notes can be difficult, especially when you're spending half of the day listening to a lecture.

When your bar prep classes are over, you will have an additional three or four hours each day in which to study. You will be amazed at how much you can learn during this extra time.

Upon entering the final weeks before the bar exam, you should have all your study materials completed or nearly completed. In the final weeks before the bar exam, you need to concentrate on memorizing your notes, outlines and/or flashcards. If you already have a subject wired, limit review of that subject to *maintenance review only* and focus on subjects with which you are having more difficulty.

Continue practice testing

Practice testing is critical to help you solidify what you have been learning. It is also important because, as mentioned earlier, it helps you get used to the time pressure of bar examination.

If you have not yet taken a full-blown bar exam practice test, **do it now**. Select two days during the second to last week before the bar exam during which you will do a practice bar exam.

If you have already done a full-blown practice bar exam, you still need to continue with mini practice tests. That is, you should write a few essays under timed conditions with no notes, take blocks of MBE questions under timed conditions (e.g., answer 50 MBE questions in 1.5 hours), and write out at least one performance test under timed conditions.

It is possible that you have already written out numerous performance tests and essays. If you're to the point where you no longer feel that writing out a complete answer is of any value to you, use your time to practice outlining answers so that you continue to hone your issue-spotting skills.

Adjust your sleep schedule

It is my belief that you should generally study for the bar exam during the hours in which the bar exam is administered in order to train your body and mind to perform at peak levels at the proper time. In short, your bar exam studies would ideally occur between 8:00 a.m. and 5:00 p.m.

Based on what I know of reality, however, many people study late into the night. If this works for you, great. Unfortunately, you can't take the bar exam at 10:00 p.m., so you will need to adjust your sleep schedule in order to be awake and alert during the two or three days of the bar exam when you will be expected to perform during "regular business hours."

Unless you are one of those rare people who can fall asleep at any time of day, you will need to start adjusting your sleep schedule now so that waking up at 6:00 a.m. and being ready to start the bar examination at 8:00 a.m. won't kill you.

Probably the easiest way to adjust your sleep schedule is to begin going to sleep 15 to 30 minutes earlier each day until you're going to sleep at an appropriate time, such as 10:00 p.m., to allow yourself to wake up around 6:00 a.m.

Confirm your examination arrangements

Now is not the time to be worrying about how you will get to the bar exam testing site or what hotel you will be staying in. If you do have these worries, get them out of the way as soon as possible so you can concentrate on memorizing and practicing.

If you are not staying at a hotel near the bar examination site, make and/or confirm arrangements for getting to the bar exam site each day. Will you drive yourself? Is a friend driving you? Do you have a backup plan if someone gets sick or your car breaks down? If you are taking public transit, do you know the route you will take and any transfers you need to make? Figure this all out now.

If you will be staying at a hotel, consider packing your suitcase now with all the clothes and supplies (pencils, pens, erasers, watch, earplugs, etc.) you will need for the test. Then, double-check your suitcase the night before you leave for the hotel to make sure you didn't forget anything. Consider what sort of snack foods you will want to have with you at the hotel, and make a shopping list for those foods.

If you will be using a laptop to take the bar exam, install and *test* your bar exam software. If for some reason you have a compatibility problem with the software, you will still have plenty of time to fix it or buy a new computer.

Finally, if you are going to be taking the bar exam somewhere you have never been before, check out Google Street View on Google Maps to get the "lay of the land." You can take a virtual tour of the area around your hotel and the testing center. If you will be walking to the testing site from your hotel, you can trace the route on the Street View.

Keep stress down

The overriding goal of my blog, Bar Exam Mind, is to help you reduce your bar exam stress. If you have a particular concern that is causing you stress or anxiety, search the blog and you should find an answer. Or, pick up a copy of the *Bar Exam Mind* book for a comprehensive review of ways to combat stress and anxiety.

Tips for Bar Exam Test Days

THIS CHAPTER CONTAINS a list of bar exam test day advice. Everyone is different, so read through this chapter, take what you think is helpful, and forget about the rest. We've all heard the story about the woman who was in labor for the last few hours of the bar exam and passed, so do what you need to do.

Where to stay

I am a believer in staying at a hotel near the testing site. If the bar exam is being held at a convention center with an attached hotel, try to stay at a different hotel. Will you fail the bar if you stay at the same hotel as the majority of takers? Not if you have studied. However, staying at a hotel with a bunch of stressed-out people, some of whom are only now starting to realize that they did not study enough and are likely going to fail, is not pleasant.

The hotel you choose should be reputable enough to guarantee a clean room and responsive staff if there is a problem. It should also be close enough to the test site that you can walk or would be able to walk to the site if, for instance, your car will not start.

When I took the bar in Oregon, the test site was a horrid old hotel near the Portland airport. The rooms were small and noisy – my room had an air conditioner that sounded like an out-of-tune V-8 engine. I could hear people pacing the hallway outside my door in the middle of the night. They were reviewing their notes and muttering to themselves. It was utter insanity. Add to that a decent level of stress and anxiety, and I probably only slept 3 hours the first night of the exam.

Not good.

Flash forward a couple years to the California bar. I took the bar exam in downtown San Diego. Fearing a repeat of my Oregon experience, I did not want to stay at the "test hotel." I looked for nearby hotels in downtown San Diego, but all were either full or exorbitantly expensive. With some trepidation, I booked a room at the test hotel. It turned out to be fine. With the exception of a few police sirens and the surprisingly loud San Diego Trolley rolling by late at night, there was little noise.

So, stay at a hotel, preferably one near the test site, but not, if you can avoid it, the hotel designated by the bar as having the "special bar exam discount rate."

Don't impose on yourself the added stress of worrying about getting stuck in

traffic or about your car breaking down . . .
stay in a hotel, even if you think you can't
afford it.

Arrive early to your hotel

If check-in time at the hotel is 2:00 p.m.,
try get there around 2:00 p.m. Then, set up
camp in your room. Make sure everything is
comfortable. Unpack your clothes and arrange
them.

You should not study anymore. You
know enough.

If you are in an urban area, get out of the
hotel and explore. See a movie. Maybe a
friend, spouse, significant other, or relative
(anyone who is *not* taking the bar) can drop
you off at the hotel and stick around to see a
movie and have dinner with you. This will
help ease your mind.

By 7:00 p.m., you should be alone. Take a
few moments to plan out tomorrow (the first

day of the exam) and arrange everything you will need. Double check your supplies and then forget about it. Watch TV or read some fiction until 9:00 or 10:00, and then turn off the lights and sleep.

Some of you will have a hard time sleeping. I don't think I ever got more than 6 hours of sleep on any exam night. That is why it is important to lie down and try to sleep. Don't stay up until 3:00 a.m. because "you're keyed up." You may be able to survive the first exam day on adrenaline and coffee, but the second day or third day may become a struggle.

What to bring to the testing site

This will depend on your jurisdiction. Most jurisdictions will allow you to bring a laptop, pens, pencils, a watch or clock, and oftentimes a pillow to use as cushioning for the extremely uncomfortable chairs that seem to plague bar exam administrations.

Some jurisdictions will allow you to bring in food and drinks. This was the case with the Oregon bar at the time that I took it. The California bar examiners are much more uptight: no food or drink inside the examination room. You must place all of your testing supplies in a tiny plastic bag and leave your backpack or other bag outside of the examination room. Nevertheless, you may bring food and drink if you leave it in your backpack. Therefore, if you get hungry or thirsty, you must stand up, exit the examination room and go to your backpack in order to eat or drink.

Moral of the story: Read your jurisdiction's rules and bring what you need.

In addition to any snacks (such as almonds, walnuts, energy bars, etc.) or drinks, you need to bring all the tools necessary to take the bar examination. Therefore, you will need to bring your pens, pencils, laptop computer, and watch or clock (for keeping time).

And don't forget to think about what you will wear on exam day. If you are taking the bar exam in a cold climate, dress in layers so you can cool down once inside the heated exam area. If you are taking the exam during the summer, don't forget to bring a sweatshirt or light jacket in case you get seated directly below an ice cold air conditioner vent.

Taking breaks

Please do not underestimate the power of taking breaks during the examination.

Unless you are an automaton, I suggest getting out of the examination room in order to relax and clear your head. I recommend leaving the examination room for a couple of minutes in order to refresh yourself at least once per testing period (e.g., at about 45 minutes during a 90 minute testing block).

Please note that this is controversial advice. I have had some readers of my blog say that I am insane to suggest this. So, make your own decision.

If you decide to take breaks, you might, for example, complete two of three essays and then get up from your spot, walk outside of the examination room, and get a quick drink of water, eat something, or go to the bathroom, before returning to your seat and working on the next essay.

I made sure to take breaks both times I took the bar exam. A little break like this serves two purposes: (1) it allows you to stretch your legs and replenish your body's energy reserves and (2) allows you to take your mind off what you just worked on and change to a new topic.

Also, if you are working on an essay or PT and are drawing a total blank and there is no other task to move on to, get up and take a break. If you can get near some windows, look out at the trees, grass, buildings, cars, people . . . whatever is outside. Take deep breaths to help get oxygen to your body and brain. This should help clear your head and get your mind working again to enable you to respond to the question at hand.

During the MBE, I always took at least one break around the 50-question point. I would recommend doing at least that, though a break after each third of the test (at 33 and 66 questions) would probably be ideal because you would be getting up and stretching each hour.

Finally, for those of you who feel you absolutely cannot spare five minutes to get up and leave the testing area, at least take a one-minute mental break. Sit back, close your eyes, and think about something other than the bar exam: the ocean, your favorite food, your significant other, nothingness, etc. Just try to focus on something else and relax.

Refocusing during the exam

I don't think humans are meant to sit and do anything for three hours straight, much less stare at black squiggles on a computer screen or paper. But, if you are able to focus for that long, then by all means, do it!

For those of you who are like me and whose attention can drift more easily, here is my suggestion: If you find yourself losing focus during the bar exam, then ... lose focus.

What I mean is, turn your attention to something else for 1-2 minutes. You can do this by taking a quick drink or bathroom break, as already discussed. Or, you could just stare up at the ceiling or at your fingernails.

(Just be careful not to start accidently staring at someone else's answer sheet!)

You can also try a mini-meditation: Close your eyes. Breathe in and out slowly. Focus all of your attention on each breath. Do this 10 times. You should feel much more focused.

Losing focus is your mind's way of telling you: "I'm freaking bored!" So, change the subject of your attention for a brief period, and you should be refreshed and ready to go . . . at least for an hour or so when it will be time for another quick break.

Lunchtime

The day of your arrival at your hotel, you should locate two or three restaurants near the test site that look like they serve a good lunch. You need to choose multiple restaurants in case one is extremely crowded.

When you get lunch, I would advise ordering something that is fully cooked and avoiding any cut fruits or uncooked vegetables unless you are eating a washed, unsliced apple or a banana or something similar. Call this paranoia, but it would be awful to fail the bar examination because you're in your hotel room vomiting continuously due to some sort of food borne pathogen.

An even better option would be to bring food from your home and keep it in your hotel room and then return to the hotel room for lunch. (You might also consider pre-ordering breakfast and lunch room service so food is waiting at the hotel room in the morning before the exam and during the lunch break.)

I brought my lunch for the first day of the Oregon bar exam, and I think it was a good idea. The benefit is that eating lunch in your hotel room by yourself allows you to stretch out on your bed and relax while avoiding the crush of anxious bar examinees in the restaurants who are wolfing down a sandwich and convincing themselves by speaking out loud that they just failed the bar exam because they did not know a single answer during the morning session. Avoid such people, talk and thoughts.

My choice for lunch out during the bar exam is a grilled chicken sandwich or chicken burrito, a banana or an apple, a couple glasses of water, and a cup of coffee (to keep the energy up).

NOTE: If you are a vegetarian or a vegan, you will need to be especially diligent with preparing for your meals. Make sure you have that figured out well in advance so that it does not become another source of stress during the bar exam itself. Maybe a friend or relative could bring you lunch each day.

Nighttime

After you complete the afternoon session of the examination, go back to your hotel room and relax for at least 30 minutes. If you're a bit stressed out about your answers, feel free to run through them in your mind, but do not obsess about them. Once the 30 minutes is up, try to completely forget about the test that day.

Your mind needs to relax so it can be ready for the next day.

Go out and get some dinner (same rules for food choices apply from lunchtime). If you are a drinker, treat yourself to a glass of beer or wine, but no more than one. If you're staying in a hotel nearby attractions such a mall or a waterfront or a movie theater, take advantage of them.

Be sure that you are back in your hotel room by 9:00 p.m. Organize the supplies that you will need for the next day of the exam. I would advise not reviewing any notes, outlines, or flashcards. If you feel you simply must do some review, I would advise doing it before 8:00 p.m., that way your brain can have a chance to slow down and relax for a couple hours before you go to sleep.

Then, be ready to do it all over again the next day!

Conclusion

I HOPE YOU FOUND *Bar Exam Basics* to be helpful for your bar exam preparations. Whether or not you implement some or all of my suggestions, I am sure you will do well on the bar exam.

Please let me know what you thought of this book by writing a review where you purchased it or by sending me a comment via my blog's contact page at *barexammind.com/contact.*

If you need more help with your bar exam preparation, be sure to check out the other books in the *Pass the Bar Exam Series*:

Book 2: *How to Write Bar Exam Essays: Strategies and Tactics to Help You Pass the Bar Exam*

Book 3: *Bar Exam Mind: A Strategy Guide for an Anxiety-Free Bar Exam*
Book 4: *The Bar Exam Mind Bar Exam Journal*

And be sure to check out the other bar exam products available on BarExamMind.com:

- MBE Outlines
- California Bar Outlines

Good luck on the bar exam!